THE

ASIAN

— WORLD —

600–1500

STUDENT STUDY GUIDE

OXFORD
UNIVERSITY PRESS

Oxford University Press, Inc., publishes works that
further Oxford University's objective of excellence
in research, scholarship, and education.

Oxford   New York
Auckland   Cape Town   Dar es Salaam   Hong Kong   Karachi
Kuala Lumpur   Madrid   Melbourne   Mexico City   Nairobi
New Delhi   Shanghai   Taipei   Toronto

With offices in
Argentina   Austria   Brazil   Chile   Czech Republic   France   Greece
Guatemala   Hungary   Italy   Japan   Poland   Portugal   Singapore
South Korea   Switzerland   Thailand   Turkey   Ukraine   Vietnam

Published by Oxford University Press, Inc.
198 Madison Avenue, New York, NY 10016
www.oup.com

ISBN 978-0-19-522262-3 (California edition)   ISBN 978-0-19-522340-8

Project Director: Jacqueline A. Ball
Education Consultant: Diane L. Brooks, Ed.D.
Design: designlabnyc

Casper Grathwohl, Publisher

Printed in the United States of America
on acid-free paper

Dear Parents, Guardians, and Students:

This study guide has been created to increase student enjoyment and understanding of *The Asian World, 600–1500*. It has been developed to help students access the text. As they do so, they can learn history and the social sciences and improve reading, language arts, and study skills.

The study guide offers a wide variety of interactive exercises to support every chapter. Parents or other family members can participate in activities labeled "With a Parent or Partner." Adults can help in other ways, too. One important way is to encourage students to create and use a history journal as they work through the exercises in the guide. The journal can simply be an off-the-shelf notebook or three-ring binder used only for this purpose. Some students might like to customize their journals with markers, colored paper, drawings, or computer graphics. No matter what it looks like, a journal is a student's very own place to organize thoughts, practice writing, and make notes on important information. It will serve as a personal report of ongoing progress that your child's teacher can evaluate regularly. When completed, it will be a source of satisfaction and accomplishment for your child.

Sincerely,

Casper Grathwohl
Publisher

This book belongs to:

_____

CONTENTS

HOW TO USE THE STUDENT STUDY GUIDES TO
THE MEDIEVAL & EARLY MODERN WORLD

Each book in The Medieval & Early Modern World *introduces you to compelling adventures of fascinating men and women living at an amazing time. You will meet artists and warriors, rulers and scientists, merchants, traders, and slaves. You'll experience their lives close up, through diaries, letters, poems, songs, and myths.*

The events of the medieval and early modern time period changed the whole world forever. The foundations of international politics, the boundaries of countries and empires, the roots of educational and religious institutions—all were established during this rich, electrifying period. We can't fully understand our world today without understanding how it connects with these times.

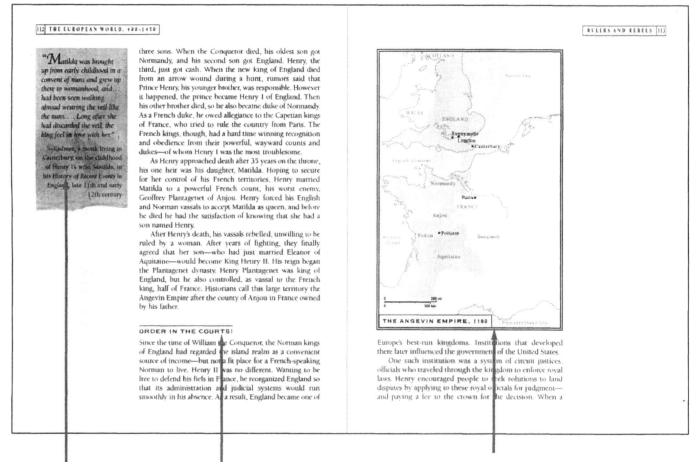

Short quotes in sidebars tell about life in the words of someone living at the time.

Subheads give clues to the content to follow.

Geography has a lot to do with history. Maps show the locations of important places and supply a geographic context for important events.

This study guide will help you as you read the books in the series. It will help you learn and enjoy history while building thinking and writing skills. And it will help you pass important tests. The sample pages below show the books' special features. But before you begin reading the book or using this guide, be sure to have a notebook or extra paper and a pen handy to make a history journal. A dictionary and thesaurus will help you too. A special tip: Before you start a new chapter, read the two-part chapter title and predict what you will learn from the chapter. Check to see if you were right at the end.

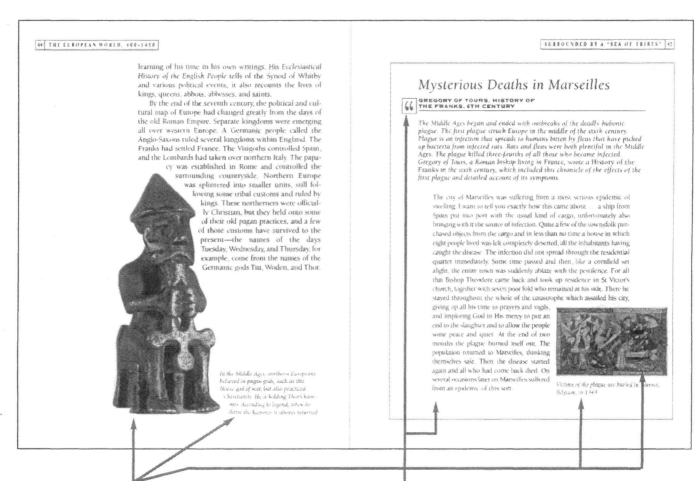

Pictures, often of artifacts, show art and design of the times. Read the captions to learn even more than is in the text.

Every chapter has a long primary source quote that takes you back in time to the scene of an important action in a dramatic, powerful, first-person way. Look for these longer quotations marked by quotation marks followed by the source of the work.

On the next pages you will find models of graphic organizers. You will need these to do the activities for each chapter on the pages after that. Go back to the book as often as you need to.

GRAPHIC ORGANIZERS

As you read and study history, geography, and the social sciences, you'll start to collect a lot of information. Using a graphic organizer is one way to make information clearer and easier to understand. You can choose from different types of organizers, depending on the information.

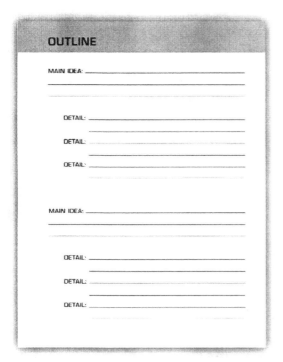

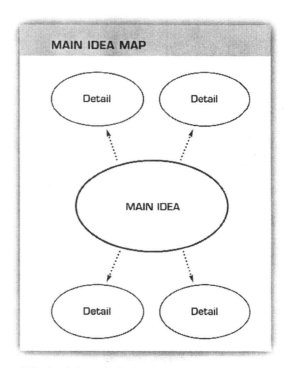

Outline

To build an outline, first identify your main idea. Write this at the top. Then, in the lines below, list the details that support the main idea. Keep adding main ideas and details as you need to.

Main Idea Map

Write down your main idea in the central circle. Write details in the connecting circles.

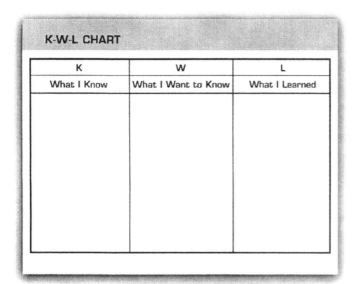

K-W-L Chart

Before you read a chapter, write down what you already know about a subject in the left column. Then write what you want to know in the center column. Then write what you learned in the last column. You can make a two-column version of this. Write what you know in the left and what you learned after reading the chapter.

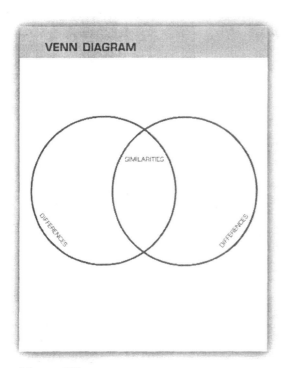

Venn Diagram

These overlapping circles show differences and similarities among topics. Each topic is shown as a circle. Any details the topics have in common go in the areas where those circles overlap. List the differences where the circles do not overlap.

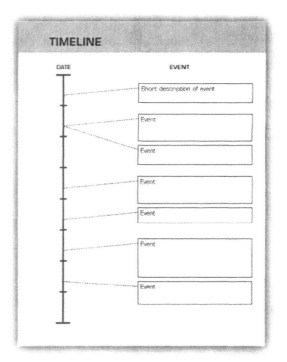

Timeline

A timeline divides a time period into equal chunks of time. Then it shows when events happened during that time. Decide how to divide up the timeline. Then write events in the boxes to the right when they happened. Connect them to the date line.

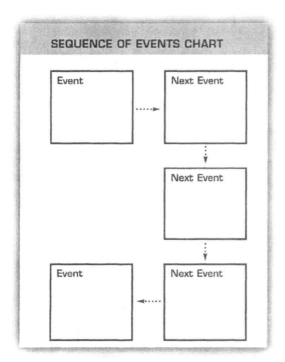

Sequence of Events Chart

Historical events bring about changes. These result in other events and changes. A sequence of events chart uses linked boxes to show how one event leads to another, and then another.

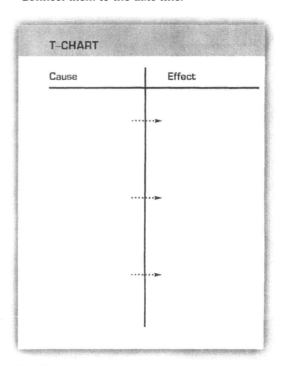

T–Chart

Use this chart to separate information into two columns. To separate causes and effects, list events, or causes, in one column. In the other column, list the change, or effect, each event brought about.

REPORTS AND SPECIAL PROJECTS

There's always more to find about the years 600–1500, the period of time covered by *The Asian World*. Take a look at the Further Reading section at the end of the book. Here you'll find a number of books that can extend and enrich your study of this time of Mongols, Mughals, samurai, shoguns, kings and khans.

GETTING STARTED

Explore the Further Reading section for any of these reasons:

▶ You're curious and want to learn more about a particular topic.

▶ You still have questions about something covered in the book.

▶ You need more information for a research or other classroom project.

What's the best way to find the books that will help you the most?

LOOK AT THE SUBHEADS

The books are organized by topic. For example, the subhead "Biography" will tell you where to read the life stories of both Khubilai and Genghis Khan, Marco Polo, and the travelers along the Silk Road. Other subheads direct you to books on specific countries, kingdoms, and topics, like Warfare, Science, Folktales and Art.

LOOK AT THE BOOK TITLES

Browse through the list of book titles as if you were in a library or bookstore. Book titles often give clues to not only the main topic covered inside, but also to the way an author approaches the subject. For example, just by reading the title, you can tell that *The Silk Route: 7,000 Miles of History* and *The Silk Road: Art and History* will tell the story of the Silk Road from different angles.

LOOK FOR GENERAL REFERENCES

General references are always a good place to start when you are exploring a new subject, since they will include some information about lots of topics related to your interest. The books listed under "Dictionaries and Encyclopedias" are all good general references. Look under the subhead for the country, too. Also look for "Atlases" and "Primary Source Collections."

OTHER RESOURCES

Information comes in all kinds of formats. Use the book to learn about primary sources. Go to the library for videos, DVDs, and audio materials. And don't forget about the Internet.

PRIMARY SOURCES

The titles marked by quotation marks are primary sources. Flip through your student book and make a list of primary sources in the text. You can easily find translations or other versions of many of these in your school or local library. Think up your own writing projects based on this material.

AUDIO-VISUAL MATERIALS

Your school or local library can offer documentary videos and DVDs on on this period of history, as well as audio materials. If you have access to a computer, explore the sites listed in the section titled Websites (just before the Index) for some good jumping-off points. These are organized by topic, with brief descriptions of what you'll find on the site. Many websites list additional reading as well as other Internet links you can visit.

What you've found out about *The Asian World* so far is just a beginning. Learn more to be part of an ongoing adventure. Use the library/media center research log to guide and focus your research.

TWO TEACHERS: BUDDHA, KONGZI, AND EARLY INDIA AND CHINA

CHAPTER SUMMARY

In the 6th century BCE two new religions developed in India and China: Buddhism and Kongzi, or Confucianism. Other religions and philosophies included Daoism, Legalism, Jainism, and Brahmanism (later called Hinduism). As India and China traded with other countries, they spread their religions. Buddhism became one of the world's leading religions.

ACCESS

What do you know about the religions that are the main topic of this chapter? What would you like to know? Fill out a K-W-L chart. Use the graphic organizer your teacher gives you, or copy the chart on page 8 of this study guide. Write some facts you know about Buddhism, Confucianism, and Hinduism in the first column. (If you don't know anything about one or more of these religions, that's fine. Just leave the column blank.) In the second column, write what you would like to learn. After you read the chapter, fill in the final column, which is what you learned.

CAST OF CHARACTERS

Write a few sentences explaining why each person is important.

Siddartha Gautama (sid-AR-tha Gow-TA-ma)

_____

_____

Kong Zhongni (koong joong-nee)

_____

_____

Laozi (laow-dzuh)

_____

_____

Qin Shi Huangdi (chin sher hwong-dee)

_____

_____

Mahavira (MA-ha-VEE-ra)

_____

_____

Ashoka (uh-SHOK-uh)

_____

_____

Emperor Wu

_____

_____

WORD BANK

nomadic meditate frugally rituals radical exploitation subcontinent

Choose a word from the Word Bank to complete each sentence. One word is not used.

1. Overcharging poor people who can't shop elsewhere is _____ .

2. Some people _____ daily to calm their mind.

3. No one knew where to send the letter because the family is _____ .

4. Church services include _____ that are the same every Sunday.

5. Have you ever visited the Indian _____?

6. The janitor saved money for her retirement because she lived _____ .

WORD PLAY

Look up the word you did not use in the dictionary. Which meaning of the word is the one that was used in the chapter? Write a sentence that uses that meaning of the word.

_____

WITH A PARENT OR PARTNER

With the help of a family member or another partner, research Siddartha Gautama. Find information about the life and accomplishments of Siddartha, the founder of Buddhism, on the Internet or in a print biography. Jot down some important points. Then share what you learned with other family members or friends.

CRITICAL THINKING
DRAWING CONCLUSIONS

Use your background knowledge and thinking skills, as well as information from the chapter, to answer the questions below.

1. How unusual a person was Siddartha Gautama? Give reasons for your answer.

_____

_____

_____

2. What would be some important qualities of an ideal society according to Kongzi?

_____

_____

_____

3. Why was using written merit exams to pick public officials such a radical idea in China during the Han period?

_____

_____

_____

CRITICAL THINKING

COMPARE AND CONTRAST

Following is a list of words and phrases related to Buddhism and Hinduism. Organize them into the Venn diagram provided. Write the corresponding letter of the words or phrases that relate to Buddhism into the circle labeled *Buddhism*. Write the corresponding letter of the words or phrases that describe Hinduism in the circle labeled *Hinduism*. Any words or phrases common to both religions belong in the area where the circles overlap.

a. began in India
b. based on the belief of many gods
c. spread to China
d. emphasizes truth and duty
e. believes in the caste system
f. built temples
g. emphasizes living with virtue
h. founded by a prince
i. emerged from an ancient religion

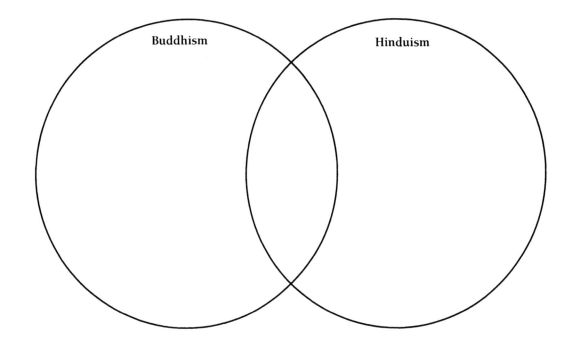

WRITE ABOUT IT

Suppose that you are a disciple, or follower, of the Buddha who was chosen to spend a day with him. What was the day like? What did you do, and how did you feel about it? Write a few paragraphs describing your actions and impressions.

_____

_____

_____

_____

_____

WORKING WITH PRIMARY SOURCES

Read the following excerpt from the Lotus Sutra (about 100 CE). Then answer the following questions.

> When I hear the Buddha's gentle voice,
>
> Profound, far removed from the ordinary understanding,
>
> > extremely subtle,
>
> Setting forth the pure Dharma,
>
> > My heart is overjoyed.
>
> My doubts and second thoughts are cleared away forever,
>
> > And I dwell securely in the midst of real knowledge, saying:
>
> "Of a certainty I shall become a Buddha,
>
> > Revered by gods and men."

1. A follower of the Buddha wrote these verses. How did the person feel about the Buddha?

_____

_____

2. What is dharma, and what happens to believers who follow the dharma? Look back in the chapter if you don't remember.

_____

_____

3. According to the introduction, what was one important effect of the Lotus Sutra?

_____

_____

GROUP TOGETHER

Wouldn't it be interesting to talk with other students about Buddhism and Hinduism? Do you see evidence of these religions where you live? How do their values relate to the world today? Get a few friends together and ask your teacher to help you organize a discussion group at school. Have one person take notes and another person present the group's ideas to the class.

CHINA UNITED, AGAIN:
THE SUI AND TANG DYNASTIES

CHAPTER SUMMARY

Yang Jian of the Sui dynasty reunited China in 589. In 618 Li Yuan led a rebellion and proclaimed the Tang dynasty. Li's son Li Shimin, one of China's best emperors, enacted educational, tax, and land reforms. Buddhism encouraged the discovery of printing and made drinking tea popular. Poetry flourished. Tang emperors expanded the empire. Wu Zhao became the only female emperor in Chinese history. The Tang dynasty weakened and finally fell in 907.

ACCESS

Some people just don't follow the rules. Wu Zhao, whom you will read about in this chapter, was one of those people. No other woman before her time—or after—became emperor of China. What qualities do you think this exceptional person had? How did she achieve her goal? Jot down a few guesses in your journal. Then compare your ideas to the author's description of Wu Zhao.

CAST OF CHARACTERS

Write a few sentences explaining why each person is important.

Sui Wendi (sway one-dee), personal name Yang Jian (yahng jen)

_____

Li Yuan (lee yooann) _____

_____

Tang Taizong (tahng tie-dzoong), personal name Li Shimin (lee sher-min)

_____

Xuanzang (syuan-dzahng) _____

_____

Wu Zhao (woo jao) _____

_____

Tang Zuanzong (tahng syuan-dzoong)

_____

_____

Wang Wei (wong way) _____

_____

Li Bai (lee buy) _____

_____

Du Fu (doo foo) _____

_____

WORD BANK

famine stroke imperial campaign conspiracy regent regime

Choose a word from the Word Bank to complete each sentence. One word is not used.

1. A _____ ruled China because the emperor was only eight years old.

2. The _____ was so brutal that it was eventually overthrown.

3. Soldiers may be away for years on a faraway foreign _____.

4. In the third year of the _____ millions of people died.

5. The emperor's _____ robes never failed to impress his subjects.

6. After his _____ the emperor could not talk or write.

WORD PLAY

Look up the word you did not use in the dictionary. Then write a noun, a verb, and an adjective with the same base.

_____

WITH A PARENT OR PARTNER

Work with a family member or another partner to construct a timeline of the Sui and Tang dynasties. Show when each dynasty began and when it ended. Decide together which other important events to include on the timeline. You can use the timeline to review the information you read in the chapter.

CRITICAL THINKING
COMPARE AND CONTRAST

Draw a Venn diagram in your history journal (copy the diagram on page 9 of this study guide). On the diagram, compare and contrast two of the emperors in this chapter. Write the name of each emperor over one of the circles. Note the ways that the emperors were similar in the overlapping part of the circles. Then use the diagram to help you write a short comparison of the emperors on the lines below.

_____
_____
_____
_____
_____

DRAWING CONCLUSIONS

Use what you know about people's behavior and what you learned in the chapter to speculate about Wu Zhao's rule. Explain why you believe the people of China did not rebel when Wu Zhao proclaimed herself emperor in 690.

_____
_____
_____
_____
_____

WORKING WITH PRIMARY SOURCES

Remember the excerpt from *The Life of Xuanzang* that was read aloud to you? Read the last paragraph of that excerpt below. Then answer the questions.

No warning. It had been a spring day like any other. Xuanzang and his **entourage** descend from the **vale of Kashmir** to find their way down to the great . . . **Gangetic plain** of north India. The setting is a forest . . . fifty robbers are lying in wait for just such a caravan. They ambush the pilgrim and his party, strip them of their clothes, steal their goods, and chase them into a dried up marsh. The former lake, enclosed by a wall of matted vines and thorns, makes an ideal pen for slaughter. The **brigands** are already beginning to tie up some caravan members when a young monk helps Xuanzang escape. The two of them get away and seek help from a village a mile away. The rescuers from the village free those who had been tied up. Everyone is shaken by the loss of their possessions and their narrow escape from death. Xuanzang alone seems untouched by what had happened. "Life is the most precious thing in existence," declares Xuanzang.

entourage, companions

vale of Kashmir, mountainous region in northern India

Gangetic plain, plain of the Ganga River in India

brigands, bandits

1. Do you think Xuanzang and his group suspected what the robbers intended to do to them after stealing their possessions?

_____

_____

_____

2. Why do you suppose Xuanzang was unruffled by this terrible experience?

_____

_____

_____

3. Would you have wanted to be a part of Xuanzang's group? Why or why not?

_____

_____

_____

WRITE ABOUT IT

Read the excerpt from the poem "Fighting South of the Wall." Then paraphrase the poet's message to the reader.

Yesterday's man on top of the wall
Beneath the wall is a ghost today.
Still the banners are like an array of stars;
And the war drums' sound is not yet done;
And out of my family, husbands and sons,
All are there in the sound of the drums.

—Tang poet Li Bai, "Fighting South of the Wall, No. 2," about 755

_____

_____

_____

_____

_____

WORKING WITH PRIMARY SOURCES

Du Fu is thought to be the greatest of Chinese poets—he is often called a god of poetry. As the Tang government was falling apart in the eighth century because of invaders and war, Du Fu lived as a poor wanderer. He wrote sad poetry about his career failures and lamented the warfare and destruction around him. Like the best Chinese poets, he tells his story by using images of nature. We look at the images he gives us to discover his feelings at being away from the center of power. A Buddhist monk named Guanxu was also writing poetry during the Tang dynasty. In the third poem here, he describes drinking tea.

Read the three poems below and answer the questions.

I. By **Yangtse** and **Han** the mountains pile their barriers.
A cloud in the wind, at the corner of the world.
Year in, year out, there's no familiar thing,
And stop after stop is the end of my road.
In ruin and discord, the Prince of Ch'in-ch'uan
Pining in exile, the courtier of Ch'u.
My heart in peaceful times had cracked already,
And I walk a road each day more desolate.

    —Du Fu

Yangtse and **Han**, major Chinese rivers

Ch'in-ch'uan, an ancient Chinese ruler
Chu, a powerful ancient Chinese state)

II. In Fuzhou, far away, my wife is watching
The moon alone tonight, and my thoughts fill
With sadness for my children, who can't think
Of me here in Chang'an; they're too young still.
Her cloud-soft hair is moist with fragrant mist.
In the clear light her white arms sense the chill.
When will we feel the moonlight dry our tears,
Leaning together on our window-sill?

    —Du Fu

II. In a deep brazier I heat an iron flask,
The tea, blended with bitter herbs is warming.
The fire, fed with cedar roots, is fragrant. . . .
A good heap of sutras is read through.

    —Guanxu

1. Describe the overall mood in each of the poems.

 _____

 _____

 _____

2. Which poet seems content with his life?_____

 Circle or underline the words or phrases in the poem that show this.

3. Which poems express longing and sorrow? _____

 Circle or underline the words or phrases in the poem that show this.

4. What specific event is reflected in the second poem by Du Fu?

 _____

 _____

 _____

CHAPTER 3

RAJAS AND SULTANS: THE STRUGGLE FOR INDIA

CHAPTER SUMMARY

India was difficult to unite because it was so diverse. Two rulers who succeeded for a time were Harsha Vardhana, who controlled most of northern India in the 7th century, and Arab prince Muhammad ibn Qasim, who conquered cities in present-day Pakistan. From the early 8th to the early 13th century, northern India endured wars, conquests, and uprisings. Much of India came to be ruled by Muslims whose ancestors had come from other places, though the common people remained Hindus.

ACCESS

India at the time covered by this chapter was very diverse, as it is today. In what kinds of discussions do you hear the word *diversity* these days? What do the words *diverse* and *diversity* suggest to you? Answer these questions in your history journal. Then, as you read the chapter, compare your ideas about diversity with the ideas the author presents.

CAST OF CHARACTERS

Write a few sentences explaining why each person is important.

Mahadeviyakka (MA-ha-DEV-ee-YAK-ka) _____

_____

Harsha Vardhana (HAR-sha var-DAHN-ha) _____

_____

Muhammad (mu-HAM-mahd) _____

_____

Muhammad ibn Qasim (mu-HAM-mahd ib-in KASS-im) _____

_____

Mahmud of Gazni (ma-MOOD of GAHZ-nee) _____

_____

Bhoj (BOE-ja) _____

_____

Muhammad Ghori (mu-HAM-mahd GORE-ee) _____

_____

Qutb-ud-Ddn Aybak (KUTB-ood-deen AYE-bahk) _____

_____

Kalidasa _____

_____

WORD BANK

realm   diverse   tolerant   access   salvation   benefactors   clarity   decisive

Choose a word from the Word Bank to complete each sentence. One word is not used.

1. Some companies are so _____ they don't have set hours or dress codes.

2. People may hope for _____ through good works or through their faith.

3. Far out in the country people may not have _____ to the Internet.

4. It took weeks to travel the Rajah's _____ .

5. Everyone understood the laws because of their _____ and non-technical vocabulary.

6. The size and inexperience of the defending army made the attacker's victory

   _____

7. Our school's _____ student body speaks over twenty languages at home.

WORD PLAY

Look up the word you did not use in the dictionary. Then write a sentence that explains the origin of the word.

_____

WITH A PARENT OR PARTNER

With a family member or another partner locate photographs of the various regions and peoples of India. Check the Internet and travel books. Compare the different parts of this enormous country. Then make a list of some of the kinds of diversity that you can and cannot see in the photographs. Discuss how diversity might have made it difficult to for one person to rule large regions of India for long periods of time.

WHAT HAPPENED WHEN?

Make a timeline with the following dates on it. Use the timeline graphic organizer that your teacher gives you or copy the one on page 9 of this study guide, adding or taking away boxes if you need to.

590   610   632   647   712   1004   1030   1173   1192

1202   1206

CRITICAL THINKING
MAKING INFERENCES

Use what you already knew, what you learned in the chapter, and common sense to answer the questions.

1. How do you think her parents felt when Mahadeviyakka decided to devote her life to Shiva? Why might they have felt that way?

   _____

   _____

2. In what way did living in Mecca affect Muhammad's beliefs?

   _____

   _____

3. What motivation might Muhammad ibn Qasim have had for respecting the local religions after he conquered the main cities of Sind?

   _____

   _____

WORKING WITH PRIMARY SOURCES

Reread the lines from poems by Mahadeviyakka that appeared in Chapter 3 of your book. Then answer the questions.

> So the immortal Lord white as jasmine is my husband:
> Take these husbands who die,
> Decay, and feed them to the kitchen fires.
>
> A vein of sapphires
> hides in the earth,
> a sweetness in fruit.
>
> And in plain-looking rock
> lies a golden ore,
> and in seeds,
> the treasure of oil.
>
> Like these,
> the Infinite
> rests concealed in the heart.
>
> No one can see the ways
> of our jasmine-white Lord.

1. According to the poem, why didn't the speaker want to marry?

   _____

   _____

2. What is similar about sapphires, fruit, plain-looking rock, and seeds?

   _____

   _____

3. To what are these things compared?

   _____

   _____

4. Why do you think verses such as these were so beloved by millions of Hindus?

   _____

   _____

WRITE ABOUT IT

Sum up the activities and influence of Muslim rulers in India.

_____

_____

_____

_____

_____

HISTORY JOURNAL

Don't forget to share your history journal with your classmates, and ask if you can see what their journals look like. You might be surprised—and get some new ideas.

WORKING WITH PRIMARY SOURCES

COMPREHENSION

Read the quotations. Then answer the questions.

> In the cool woods, where
> the bees seek flowers,
> Women, bright-bangled and
> garlanded, drink
> The sap of the palm and the
> pale sugar-cane,
> And the juice of the coconut
> which grows in the sand,
> Then running they plunge
> into the sea.
>
> — Anonymous, "A Village Festival," poem from *Eight Anthologies*, a
> collection of poems in the Tamil language of southeastern India, 6th
> century

> All subjects are dependent on their lord.
> Only well-rooted trees bear fruit,
> and only when the king is strong
> do men's works prosper.
>
> — Narayana, Indian poet, from the Hitopadesa, or "Salutary Instructions," a
> collection of poems and fables, 12th century

> The priests, of whom there are several thousands, are men of the highest
> learning and talent. . . . From morning till night they engage in discussion; the
> old and the young mutually help one another.
>
> — Chinese monk Xuanzang, visiting Nalanda University, *Journey to the West*,
> about 655.

1. What did the writer of "A Village Festival" think of the festival? How do you know?

_____

_____

_____

2. In the second excerpt, to what is a king compared?

_____

_____

_____

3. What does the speaker in the second verse believe? Do you agree?

_____

_____

_____

4. How would you describe Xuanzang's impression of Nalanda University?

_____

_____

_____

TRADE IF BY LAND AND TRADE IF SEA: MERCHANTS, RELIGION, AND IDEAS

CHAPTER SUMMARY

Beginning in the 2nd century BCE, objects and ideas traveled the Silk Road, a network of paths across China, India, and the Middle East. Another way goods and culture traveled was by maritime shipping routes that connected the Mediterranean area, India, China, and Southeast Asia. By the end of the 15th century, trade had been taken over by Europeans.

ACCESS

Some people like to have adventures when they travel such as climbing mountains, kayaking, or photographing wild animals. Some travelers on the Silk Road or the high seas in Asia had adventures whether they wanted them or not. Why do you think that was? What kinds of adventures might they have had? Use your knowledge and imagination to list some educated guesses in your history journal.

CAST OF CHARACTERS

Write a few sentences explaining why each person is important.

Ibn Sina (IB-en SEE-nah) _____

_____

_____

Airlangga (EYE-er-LANG-ga) _____

_____

_____

WORD BANK

verdant   aromatic   supple   caravan   dominated   maritime

Choose a word from the Word Bank to complete each sentence. One word is not used.

1. The camel _____ stretched into the desert for miles.

2. These days _____ trade is not the most important kind.

3. The garden is _____ in the summer, especially after it rains.

4. The smell of _____ incense spread through the temple.

5. Leather that is particularly _____ was used to make these handbags.

WORD PLAY

Write a sentence with the word you did not use. Then look up the word in the dictionary to make sure you used the word correctly.

WITH A PARENT OR PARTNER

Skim the chapter with your partner to find the trade items mentioned. Make a list, and then discuss it with your partner. Which things can your partner tell you about? Are there any items you know about that your partner does not? Circle the items that neither one of you has ever heard of or seen. Research those trade goods on the Internet, or look them up in a dictionary or encyclopedia.

CRITICAL THINKING
IDENTIFYING THE MAIN IDEA

Identify the main idea of the following paragraphs from the chapter and write it on the lines. Remember that a main idea may be stated in a sentence in the paragraph, or it may be unstated.

1. Paragraph 4 (page 57)

_____

_____

_____

2. Paragraph 7 (page 58)

_____

_____

_____

3. Paragraph 13 (page 61)

_____

_____

_____

SUPPORTING DETAILS

Now list several details that support the main idea in these paragraphs:

1. _____

_____

_____

2. _____

_____

_____

3. _____

_____

_____

WORKING WITH PRIMARY SOURCES

Reread the words of doctor, mathematician, and philosopher Ibn Sina from Chapter 4. Then answer the questions.

> I found there many rooms filled with books which were arranged in cases, row upon row. . . . I inspected the catalogue of ancient Greek authors; I saw in this collection books of which few people have heard even the names, and which I myself have never seen either before or since.

1. What did Ibn Sina describe in this quotation?

_____

_____

_____

2. How do you think Ibn Sina felt when he saw the library?

_____

_____

_____

3. How does the library prove that trade with distant places took place in Asia?

_____

_____

_____

WRITE ABOUT IT

Sum up the importance of one of the goods, ideas, beliefs, or technologies described in this chapter.

_____

_____

_____

_____

_____

GROUP TOGETHER

Wouldn't it be interesting to talk to other students about trade between Asia and Europe in medieval times? How was it different from the way we exchange goods between countries today? What do we take for granted this day and age that would have been impossible back then? Get a few friends together and ask your teacher to help you organize a discussion group at school. Have one person take notes and another person present the group's ideas to the class.

WORKING WITH PRIMARY SOURCES

Read the quotations. Then answer the questions.

> If you want to be sure to become famous,
> Let the merchant have just payment for his goods.
> If you want to create a good name for yourself, Your Majesty,
> Treat the caravan people well.

> — Yusuf Has Hajip, chancellor of the Uighur (a Turkish-speaking people) kingdom of Kashgar, in Central Asia, in *The Knowledge Befitting a Ruler*, 1070

> When the ship's people . . . have gone on shore, it is customary . . . to offer to the king daily gifts of Chinese food and wine; it is for this reason that when vessels go to Borneo they must take with them one or two good cooks.

> — Zhao Rugua, Chinese maritime official, in his book, *Records of Foreign Places*, about 1300

> [Sumatra] was verdant and beautiful, most of its trees being coco-palms, . . . clove trees, . . . mangos, . . . sweet orange trees, and camphor-canes.

> — Ibn Battuta, Arab traveler, about an island that is part of present-day Indonesia, in *Travels*, 1347

1. What are all three excerpts about?

_____

_____

_____

2. Though different people in different parts of Asia wrote the first two excerpts during different centuries, both quotations are similar in one way. What way is that?

_____

_____

_____

3. Why do you suppose Yusuf Has Hajip thought it was so important for the ruler to treat traders fairly and politely?

_____

_____

_____

_____

4. From the description in the last quote, what sort of climate do you think Sumatra had? Why?

_____

_____

_____

_____

BONES AND BUDDHISTS: EARLY KOREA AND JAPAN

CHAPTER SUMMARY

During the 6th and 7th centuries CE, Korean rulers strengthened ties with China and Japan. In the 7th century, Korea unified under one ruler and prospered for a century and a half. A new dynasty ruled for the next 450 years. In Japan Buddhism and Confucianism took hold. By the early 11th century, most of Japan's people were poor, but art and literature flourished among the aristocracy. In 1185 civil wars caused a new period to begin.

ACCESS

In this chapter, you will read about royalty in Korea and Japan long ago. In your history journal, make a list of the countries today that have kings and queens. Write down as many rulers' names as you can recall. Do you have any ideas about the duties these people perform? Jot down some ideas. As you read the chapter, compare the power and responsibilities of present-day rulers with rulers in early Korea and Japan.

CAST OF CHARACTERS

Write a few sentences explaining why each person is important.

Kim Wonjong (kim wohn-johng)

_____

_____

Sondok (sohn-duck)

_____

_____

Suiko

_____

_____

Shotoku (show-toe-koo)

_____

_____

Fujiwara Michinaga (foo-jee-wah-rah mee-chee-nah-gah)

_____

_____

Murasaki Shikibu (moo-rah-sah-kee shee-kee-boo)

_____

_____

WORD BANK

oppressing   status   aristocracy   doctrines   hybrid   lacquer   succession

Choose a word from the word bank to complete each sentence. One word is not used.

1. You can tell by their dress whether people are members of the _____ or commoners.

2. After serving time in prison, it is hard for people to regain their former _____ .

3. The order of _____ was interrupted when the prince was assassinated.

4. The harsh king was hated for _____ his subjects.

5. The woman had red _____ chopsticks in her upswept hair.

6. Some slang expressions are a _____ of two languages.

WORD PLAY

Write a sentence with the word you did not use. Then look up the word in a dictionary and write what it means in your own words.

_____

_____

_____

WITH A PARENT OR PARTNER

Read the first paragraph of the chapter aloud to a family member or a partner. The paragraph describes the king of Silla's classification of the aristocracy into ranks, each with its special rules. Discuss this system with your partner. What purpose did it serve? What sorts of classification systems do people use today? Think of school, government, and religious practices. What purpose do these systems serve? Write some ideas in your history journal.

WHAT HAPPENED WHEN?
TIMELINE

Use the timeline graphic organizer below to list all the important dates mentioned in the chapter in the order that they happened. Describe each event in the space below and draw a line to link it to the right date on the dateline. Fill out additional timeline sheets if you need to. Use your timeline to review the chapter.

WORKING WITH PRIMARY SOURCES

Read the poem by Ki no Tsurayuki and the quotation from *The Pillow Book* by Sei Shonagon. Then answer the questions.

> On a spring hillside
> I took lodging for the night;
> and as I slept
> the blossoms kept falling—
> even in the midst of my dreams.
>
> — Heian poet Ki no Tsurayuki, "Spring," about 900

> Nothing can be worse than allowing the driver of one's ox-carriage to be badly dressed.
>
> — Sei Shonagon, Heian period court lady, from her memoir, *The Pillow Book*, about 1030

1. What did the speaker describe in the poem?

   _____

   _____

   _____

2. What do you think is the theme of the poem?

   _____

   _____

   _____

3. What word would you use to describe the tone of the poem?

   _____

   _____

   _____

4. What does the second quotation reveal about the values of the person who wrote it?

   _____

   _____

   _____

   _____

WRITE ABOUT IT

Suppose that you were magically transported back in time and through space to appear before one of the rulers you read about in the chapter. You could ask that person three questions. Which ruler would you choose? What questions would you ask him or her?

   _____

   _____

   _____

   _____

   _____

WORKING WITH PRIMARY SOURCES

COMPREHENSION

Read the following quotation. Then answer the questions.

> This world, I think,
> Is indeed my world.
> Like the full moon I shine,
> Uncovered by any cloud.
>
> — Fujiwara Michinaga

1. Who was Michinaga?

   _____

2. What is the main point of his poem?

   _____

   _____

   _____

3. Why does Michinaga feel this way about his position in the world?

   _____

   _____

   _____

GROUP TOGETHER

Wouldn't it be interesting to talk with other students about life in Japan and Korea between the 4th and 9th centuries? What aspects about that time and place are similar to modern life? What customs and ways of life are very different? Get a few friends together and ask your teacher to help you organize a discussion group at school. Have one person take notes and another person present the group's ideas to the class.

HORSEMEN AND GENTLEMEN: THE SONG DYNASTY IN CHINA

CHAPTER SUMMARY

In 960 the Song dynasty was established. It controlled all of China except the north. The scholar-official class had new power, which came from education. Early in the 12th century the Song government was forced to move south to a new capital. Maritime trade expanded, new weapons used gunpowder, and new farming techniques helped grow more food. City life, art, and literature flourished. Women obeyed men, and many women had bound feet.

ACCESS

What was new and different about the Song dynasty? Keep track of the answer to this question as you read the chapter. Make a four-column chart in your history journal. Write these headings: *Ideas, Conflicts, Improvements/Inventions,* and *Art/Literature.* Add information as you read the chapter, and use the chart to review the activities and accomplishments of the Song dynasty.

CAST OF CHARACTERS

Write a few sentences explaining why each person is important.

Yelü Abaoji (YEH-lew ah-BAOW-jee)

_____

_____

Zhao Kuangyin (jao kwong-yin)

_____

_____

Zhu Xi (joo syee)

_____

_____

Fan Kuan (fahn kwahn)

_____

_____

Li Qingzhao (lee ching-jao)

_____

_____

WORD BANK

emulate masts encroach suspended catapults hermit rudders modify

Choose a word from the Word Bank to complete each sentence. One word is not used.

1. The sailors carved _____ from tall, straight trees.

2. Younger children often _____ older ones.

3. Scientists _____ their theories when new evidence comes to light.

4. Without _____, ships would be hard to steer.

5. Do you see the insect _____ in that chunk of amber?

6. Weeds can _____ so slowly that no one notices.

7. Soldiers used _____ to heave boulders over the wall.

WORD PLAY

Look up the word you did not use in the dictionary. Sum up the word history.

WITH A PARENT OR PARTNER

Read aloud to a family member or another partner the first paragraph following the heading The Pleasures of Life. With your partner, fill out the Venn diagram that your teacher gives you or copy the one on page 9 of this study guide to compare and contrast a city you know about with the cities Kaifeng and Hangzhou in China.

WHAT HAPPENED WHEN?

Write what happened on each date.

907 _____

960 _____

1038 _____

1044 _____

1126 _____

CRITICAL THINKING
MAKING INFERENCES

Make inferences by using what you read in the chapter, what you already know, and what makes sense to answer the questions below.

1. What problem did the Khitan and Tangut chiefs foresee if their people were to become more like the Song Chinese?

2. Why did tutors wait until their students' early teens to teach the meaning of books the youngsters had memorized years earlier?

3. To the Song, how tough an enemy was the Jin dynasty? Why?

4. Why did Li Qingzhao have such an independent life?

WORKING WITH PRIMARY SOURCES

Reread the following verses from pages 88 and 90 of your book. Then answer the questions below.

Fifteen years ago, beneath moonlight and flowers,
I walked with you
We composed flower-viewing poems together.
Tonight the moonlight and flowers are just the same
But how can I ever hold in my arms the same love?

— Li Qingzhao, 1132

They say lotus flowers bloom as she moves her feet,
But invisibly, beneath her skirt.
Her jade toes, tiny and slender,
Imprint her name wherever she steps.
Her pure chiffon skirt swirls in a dance.

— Ye Xiaoluan, 17th-century poet

1. How does the tone of the first poem contrast with the tone of the second poem?

_____

_____

2. What do the two poems reveal about the values of the Song dynasty?

_____

_____

3. Why do you think Ye Xiaoluan compares her toes to jade?

_____

_____

WRITE ABOUT IT

Sum up what you learned about the examination system, and explain how it led to the increased power of the scholar-official class.

_____

_____

_____

_____

_____

HISTORY JOURNAL

Don't forget to share your history journal with your classmates, and ask if you can see what their journals look like. You might be surprised—and get some new ideas.

WORKING WITH PRIMARY SOURCES

Read the quotations. Then answer the questions.

> We yearn for forests and streams because they are beautiful places. A painter
> should create with this thought in mind, and a beholder should study a painting
> with this thought in mind.
>
> > — Song landscape painter Guo Xi, in his essay "The Lofty Power of Forests
> > and Streams," about 1090

> In an instant the waiter would be back carrying three dishes forked in his left
> hand, while on his right arm from hand to shoulder he carried about twenty bowls
> doubled up, and he distributed them precisely as everyone had ordered without an
> omission or a mistake.
>
> > — Meng Yuanlao, writer on city life, in his book *Dreaming of the Splendor of
> > the Eastern Capital* [Kaifeng], 1147

1. Based on these quotes, what might be a good Song dynasty rule for every worker, from painters to waiters?

_____

_____

2. What sort of landscape paintings would Guo Xi approve of most?

_____

_____

3. Why do you think Guo Xi urged the viewer to keep beauty in mind when viewing a painting?

_____

_____

4. What was Meng Yuanlao's opinion of the waiter? How do you know?

_____

_____

CHAPTER 7

KHANS AND CONQUEST: THE MONGOL EMPIRE

CHAPTER SUMMARY

The great leader Temujin, or Genghis Khan ("Universal Leader"), united tribes of Mongolia and created a fearsome military force. He conquered parts of China, India, Persia, and Russia, but was unable to create permanent government institutions in these places. His successors extended the Empire into Eastern Europe and the Middle East. By 1253, when Khubilai Khan ruled China as emperor, the Mongol Empire was falling apart.

ACCESS

Consider the members, organization, and goals of the U.S. Army. Compare the U.S. Army to the army of Genghis Kahn, as you learn about it in this chapter. Use the Venn diagram blackline master, or copy the model on page 9 of this study guide to compare and contrast the two armies. What are the most significant ways the armies resemble and differ from one another?

CAST OF CHARACTERS

Write a few sentences explaining why each person is important.

Genghis Khan (JENG-hiz kahn) _____

_____

Ho'elun (HOH eh-luhn) _____

_____

Borte _____

_____

Qiu Chuji (chyoh choo-jee) _____

_____

Jochi (JOH-chee) _____

_____

Ogodei (OH-go-day) _____

_____

Mongke (MUNG-kay) _____

_____

Khubilai Khan (KOO-buh-lie kahn) _____

_____

Rashid al-Din (Rah-SHEED ahl-DEEN) _____

_____

WORD BANK

clan   confederation   domination   plunder   suppress   humility

Choose a word from the Word Bank to complete each sentence. One word is not used.

1. If the rebels _____ the museum, many famous artworks will be destroyed.

2. The ruler demonstrated his _____ by making his subjects pay tributes.

3. Police officers used harsh measures to _____ the riot.

4. Though rich, she showed her _____ by wearing simple clothes and living in a modest house.

5. The towns joined into a _____ to provide essential services.

WORD PLAY

Look up the word you did not use in the dictionary. Then write a sentence with the word that explains the word from the context.

_____

WITH A PARENT OR PARTNER

Work with a family member or another partner to construct a simple family tree for Genghis Khan's family. Use the chapter to gather information, and do further research if you have time. Show as many generations and as many people on the family tree as you can.

CRITICAL THINKING
FACT OR OPINION?

You know that a fact is a statement that can be proved correct or incorrect. An opinion can be neither proved nor disproved. Label each of the following phrases or sentences from the chapter as **fact** or **opinion**.

1. But Temujin not only survived, he grew up to become the most powerful leader in the history of the steppes, and conqueror of a very large portion of Asia. _____

2. Ho'elun also had a fierce determination to see her family survive. _____

3. Gradually, by raiding the herds of neighboring tribes, he built up his family's wealth of sheep, goats, and horses . . . _____

4. When he felt strong enough to deserve his father-in-law's trust . . . _____

5. In the 1180s his supporters assembled at a sacred site, Mount Burkhan, and pronounced him a khan, or chief. _____

6. The word *tribe* is often used loosely, and incorrectly, to refer to any non-Western ethnic group. _____

7. Genghis Khan's rise to world domination was made possible by the nature of tribal society. _____

8. Feeling little loyalty to his father's faithless kin who had abandoned him and his family years before . . . _____

9. The Mongol motivation for conquest was complex. _____

10. "I look upon the nation as a new-born child and I care for my soldiers as if they were my brothers . . . " _____

Write your opinion of Genghis Khan's leadership style. Support your opinion with facts you learned in the chapter.

_____

_____

WORKING WITH PRIMARY SOURCES

Reread the words of Genghis Khan that were quoted in Chapter 7. Then answer the questions.

I wear the same clothing and eat the same food as the cowherds and the horse-herders. We make the same sacrifices and we share the same riches.

As long as I can still eat food and say, "Make everyone who lives in their cities vanish," kill them all and destroy their homes. As long as I am still alive, keep up the slaughter.

1. Do you think Genghis Khan was telling the truth in the first quotation? Give reasons for your answer.

_____

_____

2. If the first quotation is not entirely accurate, why do you think Genghis Khan said these words?

_____

_____

3. What does the second quotation tell about Genghis Khan's character?

_____

_____

4. Compare the two quotations. Do you think it is unusual that someone who felt so warmly toward one group of people could have felt so merciless toward another? Why or why not?

_____

_____

WRITING

Whether for good or ill, Genghis Khan certainly changed the world. If you could speak to this notorious conqueror of Asia, what questions would pop into your mind? Write three questions.

_____

_____

_____

_____

_____

GROUP TOGETHER

Wouldn't it be interesting to talk with other students about Genghis Khan? Who are some other ruthless warleaders and conquerors you know from world history? What did they all have in common? How does Genghis Khan stand apart from them? Get a few friends together and ask your teacher to help you organize a discussion group at school. Have one person take notes and another person present the group's ideas to the class.

WORKING WITH PRIMARY SOURCES

DETERMINING POINT OF VIEW

Read the following quotations from the chapter. Then answer the questions that follow.

> The people live in black carts and white tents; they breed cattle and hunt, dress in furs and leather, and live upon fermented milk and meat.
>
> — Chinese Daoist priest Qiu Chuji, known as Changchun (Eternal Spring) describing the Mongols in the travel memoir *Journey to the West*, 1220

> They are never disobedient to orders nor do they ever break their word once it is given. They have preserved the values of earlier ages.
>
> — Chinese Daoist priest Qiu Chuji, known as Changchun (Eternal Spring) describing the Mongols in the travel memoir *Journey to the West*, 1220

> They are inhuman and beastly, monsters rather than men, thirsting for and drinking blood. . . . They are without human laws, know no comforts, and are more ferocious than lions or bears.
>
> — English historian Matthew Paris describing the Mongols in his book *A History of England*, 13th century

1. How would you describe the tone of the first two excerpts, which were written by a Chinese Daoist priest?

_____

_____

_____

2. How would you describe the tone of the third excerpt, which was written by an English historian?

_____

_____

_____

3. All three quotations describe the same people, the Mongols. How would you explain the difference between the first two quotes and the last one?

_____

_____

_____

_____

4. What would you want to know to decide whether the first two quotations or the last one were more accurate?

_____

_____

_____

_____

CHAPTER 8

SULTANS, SLAVES, AND SOUTHERNERS: THE SULTANATE OF DELHI IN INDIA

CHAPTER SUMMARY

As Islam spread into Hindu India, many styles and ideas began to change. The leadership of the Delhi sultanate changed often as new leaders emerged or took the position by force.

ACCESS

The rulers of the Delhi sultanate expanded Muslim rule and influenced Hindu India. In your history journal, copy the main idea map graphic organizer from page 8 of this study guide. In the largest circle write: *How the Muslim sultanates changed Hindu India.* Then, in the smaller circles, write facts that you learn about the Delhi sultanates as you read the chapter.

CAST OF CHARACTERS

As you read, match up each person with the correct description by writing the letter of the correct description on the line.

1. Qutb-ud-din Aybak _____
2. Iltumish _____
3. Raziya _____
4. Yakut _____
5. Ala-ud-din _____

6. Tughluq _____
7. Muhammad bin Tughluq _____
8. Abu 'Abdallah ibn Battuta _____
9. Timur Leng _____
10. Kabir _____

a. daughter of Aybak who seized the throne of Delhi from Iltumish's son, dressed like a man, and ruled Delhi until 1240, when she was murdered in battle

b. former slave who became sultan in 1316 and was possibly killed by his son

c. sultan of Delhi under whose rule India's economy grew because of the growth in the area of trading textiles

d. Moroccan world traveler who was befriended by Muhammad bin Tughluq, became his advisor, and was appointed as the sultan's ambassador to China

e. Turkish Muslim whose army attacked Delhi and had all Hindus in the city killed

f. Muslim slave-general under Muhammad Ghori who named himself the first sultan of Delhi and in four years changed northern India by introducing Muslim ideas and ways of life

g. Ethiopian slave who was romantically linked to Raziya and was appointed her principal advisor

h. illiterate Muslim poet influenced by Hindu ideas about God who criticized organized religion, preferring instead to follow the religion of the heart, and is considered a saint by both Hindus and Muslims

i. the son-in-law of Aybak, who succeeded him

j. son of Tughluq, known as "The Bloody Sultan" because of his ruthless and murderous method of ruling

WORD BANK

conscientious successive ambitious deference accommodate salvaged

Choose words from the Word Bank to complete the sentences.

1. Slaves who were _____ sometimes held high office.

2. Hindus were forced to _____ the new Islamic rule in India.

3. A ruler who pays careful attention to improving his country could be called _____.

4. Much of the Hindu temples that were destroyed could not be _____.

5. When Raziya showed _____ to a man for once, it proved to be her downfall.

6. In 300 years, Delhi was ruled by five _____ dynasties.

WORD PLAY

Look up the word *contemporary* in the dictionary. Use the noun meaning to write that word in a sentence.

_____

WITH A PARENT OR PARTNER

With a parent or partner, discuss the noun meaning of the word *contemporary*. Then work together to choose someone from history and make a list in your history journal of other people who were contemporaries of that person.

WHAT HAPPENED WHEN?

Write what happened on the line for each date below.

1210 _____

1236 _____

1240 _____

1296 _____

1316 _____

1333 _____

1336 _____

1398 _____

1316 _____

c. 1440 _____

1565 _____

CRITICAL THINKING
FACT OR OPINION?

A fact is a statement that can be proven. An opinion judges things or people, but it cannot be proved or disproved. Read the following statements from the chapter. Write the letter "F" next to each statement that is a fact and the letter "O" next to each statement that is an opinion.

_____ 1. Cows are sacred symbols of the generosity of the gods.

_____ 2. Sultan Raziya was a great monarch.

_____ 3. The fortresses and temples of Vijayanagara now lie in ruins.

_____ 4. Ala-ud-din was a conscientious ruler.

_____ 5. Ibn Battuta was appointed the sultan's ambassador to China.

ALL OVER THE MAP

LOCATION

Make the following changes to the map below to show India during the Delhi Sultanate and the Kingdom of Vijayanagara, about 1335. Then answer the following questions.

1. Use shading or a pattern to show the land controlled by the Delhi Sultanate. Key this shading to the legend.

2. Use shading or a pattern to show the land that belonged to the Kingdom of Vijayanagara. Key this shading to the legend.

3. Use an icon or symbol to indicate which area was dominated by Muslims. Key this symbol in the legend, with a label.

4. Use an icon or symbol to indicate which area was mainly Hindu. Key this symbol in the legend, with a label.

5. Which river did Timur Leng cross when he attacked Delhi in 1398?

WRITE ABOUT IT

In a short essay in your history journal, describe what happened to each of the cities shown on the map.

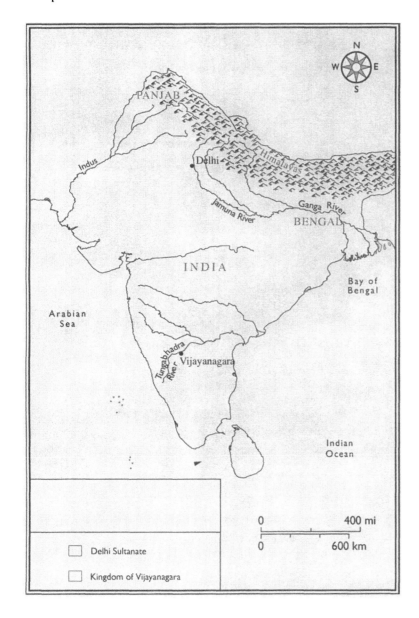

COMPREHENSION

CAUSE AND EFFECT

Complete the chart by writing the effects of the causes.

CAUSE	EFFECT
1. During Aybak's rule, Muslim styles and ways of life were affecting life in India.	
2. Raziya allowed her husband to plan a crucial battle to recover the throne for her.	
3. The Bloody Sultan appointed ibn Battuta as his ambassador to China.	
4. Vijayanagara increased its military power and weapons.	
5. Kabir, who was a Muslim greatly influenced by Hinduism, wrote poetry which helped to bring peace to Delhi.	

WORKING WITH PRIMARY SOURCES

DRAWING CONCLUSIONS

Briefly review the rulers mentioned in the chapter. Then read the quotation below from Indian Islamic writer Shaikh Hamaddani.

> In the perfection of his great wisdom, God has decreed that there be a just and competent ruler of mankind so that . . . the rules for managing the affairs of mankind might be kept and preserved on the right path.

WRITE ABOUT IT

Choose one of the rulers discussed in the chapter. Then write a paragraph explaining how this ruler fits or does not fit the description Hamaddani's definition of a just and competent ruler.

_____

_____

_____

_____

_____

CHAPTER 9

KHAN AND EMPEROR: THE YUAN DYNASTY IN CHINA

CHAPTER SUMMARY

During the reign of Khubilai Khan, the Mongol empire was expanded into Southern China and Korea, and the Grand Canal was extended. The people of China were divided along ethnic lines, and negative feelings toward the Mongols grew.

ACCESS

The success of a ruling group depends on the group's leader. Khubilai Khan was a powerful leader of the Yuan dynasty. During his reign, many positive things were accomplished, but some would argue that many negative things happened as well. Make a two-column chart in your history journal. Label the columns *positive* and *negative*. As you read, decide whether you think the facts you learn are positive or negative, and write them in the correct column on the chart.

CAST OF CHARACTERS

Explain in complete sentences why these people are important.

Marco Polo _____

_____

Khubilai Khan (KOO-buh-lie kahn) _____

_____

Liu Bingzhong (lyon bing-joong) _____

_____

Guo Shoujing (gwoh shaw-jing) _____

_____

Chabi _____

_____

Chengzong _____

_____

Renzong _____

_____

_____

WORD BANK

dynasty   cavalry   tributary

Choose words from the Word Bank to complete the sentences. One of the words is not used.

1. The Yuan _____ was founded by Khubilai Khan and lasted for almost a hundred years.

2. The Mongol _____ joined the infantry and sailors in fighting against the Song forces.

WORD PLAY

Look up in the dictionary the word that you did not use. Write that word in a sentence.

_____

WITH A PARENT OR PARTNER

Write the word bank words in your history journal. All of these words are singular nouns that end in the letter –y. Write down the plural of each word. Remember that to make a noun that ends in –y plural, the –y becomes –ies. With a parent or partner, write down as many singular nouns that end in –y as you can think of in one minute and then write the plural form. Hint: Remember that when words end with a vowel before the –y, only –s is added.

WORKING WITH PRIMARY SOURCES

DRAWING CONCLUSIONS

Ibn Battuta traveled throughout China and the East and wrote about his travels and discoveries. Read the quote from Ibn Batutta below.

The people of China of all mankind have the greatest skill and taste in the arts.

WRITE ABOUT IT

Write a paragraph giving information from the chapter that supports Ibn Batutta's statement.

_____
_____
_____
_____
_____
_____

HISTORY JOURNAL

Don't forget to share your history journal with your classmates, and ask if you can see what their journals look like. You might be surprised—and get some new ideas.

CRITICAL THINKING
SEQUENCE OF EVENTS

The sentences below describe events during the reign of Khubilai Khan. Write *before* of *after* in the blank to correctly complete each sentence. Go back to the book as often as you need to.

1. Marco Polo arrived in China _____ traveling along the Silk Road.

2. Khubilai Khan named the Yuan dynasty _____ being named the Great Khan of the Mongols.

3. Khubilai Khan came to power _____ northern China was in Mongol hands.

4. The cities of Xiangyang and Fancheng fell _____ the Song capital surrendered.

5. Khubilai Khan abolished the examination system _____ dividing the population of China into four groups

6. The southerners of China became prosperous _____ the population was divided into four groups.

7. Korea came under Mongol power _____ Khubilai Khan sent a mission to Japan.

8. Renzong was the Yuan emperor _____ Chengzong.

WITH A PARENT OR PARTNER

When you're finished, show your work to a parent or partner. Review the chapter to check your work. Then write the sentence numbers in the correct order in the the sequence of events chart below.

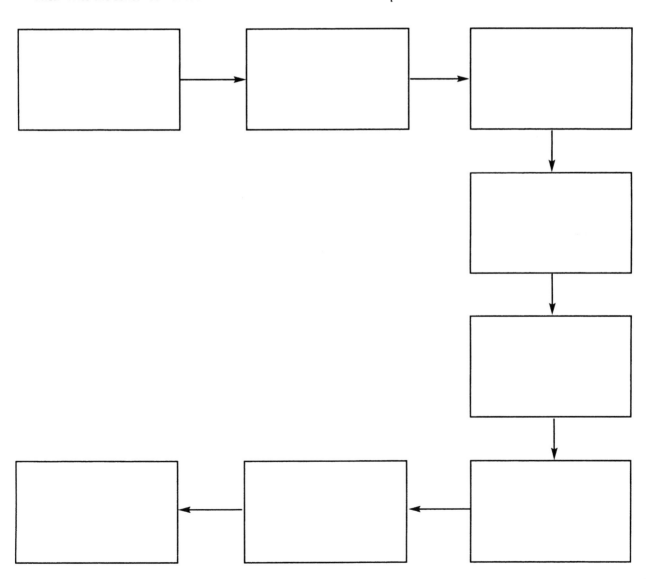

WORKING WITH PRIMARY SOURCES

Read the following passages. Then answer the questions.

> The priest has to teach religion, and the king to guarantee a rule which enables everybody to live in peace. . . . The heads of the religion and of the state are equal, though with different functions.
>
> — Tibetan Buddhist lama (monk) Phagspa, to Khubilai Khan, late 13th century

> There are four prophets who are worshipped and to whom everybody does reverence. The Christians say their God was Jesus Christ; the Saracens [Muslims] Muhammed; the Jews, Moses; and the Buddhists, Gautama Sakyamuni . . . and I do honor and reverence to all four.
>
> — Khubilai Khan

1. On the lines below, briefly summarize what each person is saying in the quotations.

_____

_____

_____

_____

_____

_____

2. Do you think that Khubilai Khan followed the advice of Phagspa? Explain.

_____

_____

_____

_____

CHAPTER 10

WARRIORS RULE: KAMAKURA AND ASHIKAGA JAPAN

CHAPTER SUMMARY

When the Minamoto clan wiped out the Taira forces in Japan, a new form of government under the shogun began to arise. At this time, new forms of Buddhism became popular.

ACCESS

What do you know about the history and culture of Japan? Write your ideas in the *Know* column of a K-W-L chart (see page 8 of this study guide). Then write questions you have about Japan in the *W*, or *What I Want to Know*, column of the chart. As you read the chapter, write answers and other new information in the *L*, or *What I Learned*, column of the chart.

CAST OF CHARACTERS

Copy the Cast of Characters into your history journal. Write two adjectives to describe each character below. Then explain why you chose these words.

Taira Kiyomori

Yoritomo

Yoshitune

Shinran

Nichiren

Godaigo

Ashikaga Takauji

Muso Soseki

WORD BANK

exiled   meditation   disciples   abdicate

Choose words from the Word Bank to complete the sentences. One word is not used.

1. The _____ of Nichiren became militant missionaries.

2. Both Shinran and Nichiren were _____ because of their ideas and beliefs.

3. Godaigo was forced to _____ his position as leader.

WORD PLAY

Look up in the dictionary the word that you did not use. Write that word in a sentence.

CRITICAL THINKING
MAIN IDEA AND SUPPORTING DETAILS

Each sentence below in italics states a main idea from the chapter. Put a check mark in the blanks in front of all of the sentences that support or tell more about the main idea.

1. *Yoritomo was a successful political leader.*

   _____ a. Yoritomo was the first of the shoguns, or generals, who would lead Japan for almost seven centuries.

   _____ b. Yoritomo established a military "tent government" which had more power than the emperor.

   _____ c. Yoritomo and his brother Yoshitsune quarreled over the victory over the Taira.

2. *Relations between China and Japan led to the development of the Zen arts in Japan.*

   _____ a. Japanese houses began to be built in the understated style of the Zen temples.

   _____ b. The Ashikaga rulers were capable rulers.

   _____ c. Gardens were built simply with stones and raked gravel.

3. *The Pure Land school [founded by Shinran] taught that you did not need to be male, study texts, or become a monk to be saved.*

   _____ a. All you had to do was take a vow of devotion to Amitabha, the Buddha of infinite light.

   _____ b. Women could become monks.

   _____ c. Shinran was exiled from the Japanese capital.

   _____ d. Evildoers had to rely on Amitabha's mercy completely.

4. *Zen Buddhism appealed to the military aristocrats.*

   _____ a. Zen taught that enlightenment comes from within, not from rituals.

   _____ b. They used Zen methods to strengthen their warrior skills.

   _____ c. Zen became closely associated with Bushido, the Way of the Warrior.

   _____ d. Students of Zen Buddhism meditated on puzzles that have no answer.

GROUP TOGETHER

Wouldn't it be interesting know what other students think about Zen Buddhism? What aspects of Zen practice would help you in an average day at school? What challenges do students face that might be helped by a Zen approach? Get a few friends together and ask your teacher to help you organize a discussion group at school. Have one person take notes and another person present the group's ideas to the class.

WORKING WITH PRIMARY SOURCES

Zen masters taught their students to meditate on questions that have no answers. Think about the following question for a minute. Can you think of an answer?

What is the sound of one hand clapping?

WRITING

Do you think the question above would be a good one to think about while meditating? Write a short paragraph explaining why or why not.

_____

_____

_____

_____

_____

_____

WHAT HAPPENED WHEN?

Describe what happened for each date below, and then draw a line to link the date to the date line.

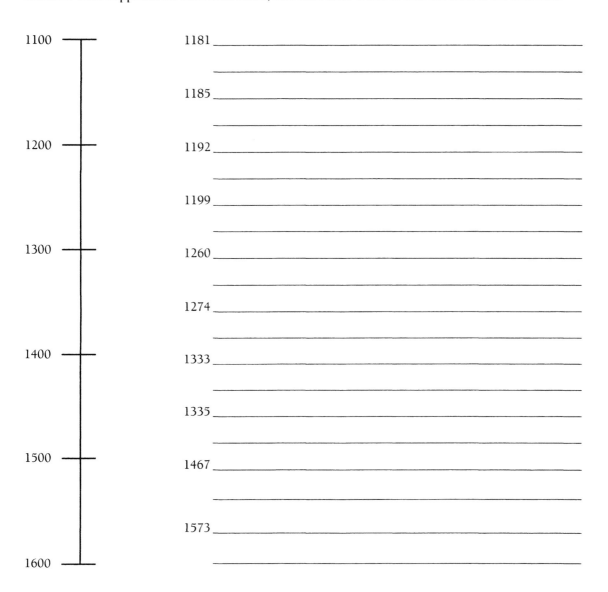

1100

1181 _____

1185 _____

1200

1192 _____

1199 _____

1300

1260 _____

1274 _____

1400

1333 _____

1335 _____

1500

1467 _____

1573 _____

1600

WORKING WITH PRIMARY SOURCES

Read the following quotations. Then answer the questions.

> For over thirty years I had tormented myself by putting up with all the things of
> this unhappy world. . . . In my fiftieth year, then, I became a priest and turned my
> back on the world.
>
> — Former aristocrat Kamo no Chomei, *An Account of My Hut*, 1212

> The law [of Buddhism] is the Truth inherent in all its perfection in every living
> creature.
>
> — Zen Buddhist master Muso Soseki, sermon at the opening of Tenryu
>   monastery, 1345

> One cannot be sure of living
> Even until the evening.
> In the dim dawn light
> I watch the waves of the wake
> Of a departing boat.
>
> — Poem by the Buddhist priest Shinkei at the time of the Onin Wars, about
>   1470

1. Which quotation relates most closely to the story of the founding of Buddhism? Explain your
   answer.

   _____

   _____

   _____

   _____

2. The third poem was written during wartime. How is this fact connected to the content of the poem?

   _____

   _____

   _____

   _____

3. What conclusions can you draw from all three poems about the Buddhist attitude toward life?

   _____

   _____

   _____

   _____

IN YOUR OWN WORDS

In your history journal, paraphrase each of these quotations, using your own words. Then write a
brief explanation of each.

WITH A PARENT OR PARTNER

The suffix *–tion* means "the act of," so *meditation* means "the act of meditating." In your history
journal, give yourself one minute to write as many words that end in *–tion* that you can think of. Ask
a parent or family member to make a list, too. Then compare lists and discuss the meaning of each
word.

FRESH DAWN:
KORYO AND EARLY CHOSON KOREA

CHAPTER SUMMARY

The rulers of Korea between 1388 and 1453 brought the country to the forefront in the areas of invention and education. Korea's relations with China allowed the country to improve in the areas of trade and intellectual development.

ACCESS

The ideas of the leaders of a country affect the way that country develops in areas of education, inventions, and relations with other countries. In your history journal, list the kings who are discussed in the chapter. As you read, write the accomplishments that occurred during each king's reign next to that person's name.

CAST OF CHARACTERS

Write why each character was important.

Yi Songgye (ee sohng-gyeh) _____

Wang Kon (wong kun) _____

Wonjong (wun-jahng) _____

T'aejong (TIE-johng) _____

Sejong (SELT-johng) _____

Munjong (MUHN-johng) _____

WORD BANK

aristocratic   besieged   unprecedented

Choose words from the Word Bank to complete the sentences. One word is not used.

1. The Mongol armies _____ the Korean town of Kuju.

2. The society of Korea was considered _____ because the people in control had power and status.

WORD PLAY

Look up in the dictionary the word that you did not use. Write that word in a sentence.

_____

WITH A PARENT OR PARTNER

The prefix *un–* makes the word it is attached to have the opposite meaning. Make a list of as many words that begin with the prefix *–un* as you can think of in one minute. Ask a parent or partner to make a list also. Then compare your lists and discuss the original word and how its meaning changes when *–un* is added.

WHAT HAPPENED WHEN?

Write a sentence stating what happened on each date. Then draw a line to connect the event to the correct date on the date line.

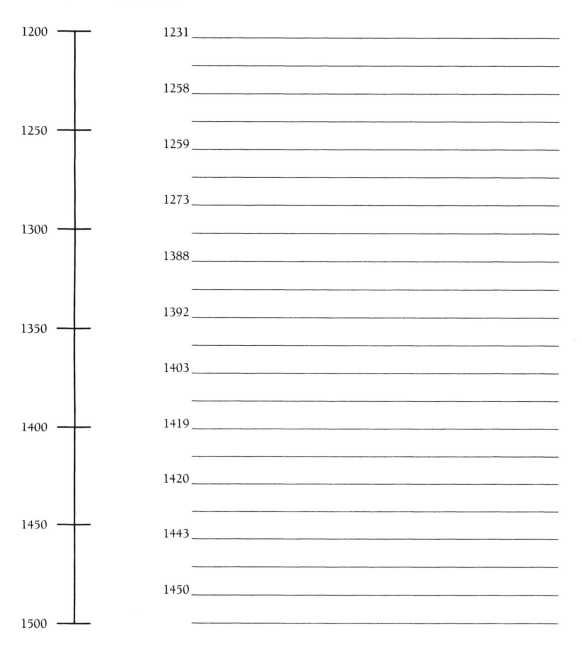

1200

1250

1300

1350

1400

1450

1500

1231 _____

_____

1258 _____

_____

1259 _____

_____

1273 _____

_____

1388 _____

_____

1392 _____

_____

1403 _____

_____

1419 _____

_____

1420 _____

_____

1443 _____

_____

1450 _____

_____

CRITICAL THINKING
CAUSE AND EFFECT

Write the letter of the effect that goes with each cause.

Causes

_____ 1.   General Yi knew his army could not win in China

_____ 2.   The Koreans killed a Mongol ambassador.

_____ 3.   The Koreans wanted to make a symbolic gesture acknowledging Ming authority.

_____ 4.   King T'aejong was not satisfied with wood-block printing.

_____ 5.   Sejong did not like that many Koreans used Chinese characters to write Korean.

Effects

a.   The Mongols attacked Koryo.

b.   He appointed a committee of scholars to create a new Korean script.

c.   He encouraged the creation of a Korean publishing industry.

d.   He seized the Korean capital and founded a new dynasty.

e.   Korea adopted a new calendar.

WITH A PARENT OR PARTNER

When you have finished the exercise, read each cause-and-effect pair aloud to a parent or partner. Link the causes and effects by inserting the word *because* at the start of each cause statement. Review any that don't sound right, and work with your partner to correct them.

WORKING WITH PRIMARY SOURCES

Read the quotation from King T'aejo regarding his ideas about why he was king.

> . . . people's wishes are such that heaven's will is clearly manifested in them; and no one should refuse the wishes of the people, for that would be to act contrary to the will of heaven.

WRITING

Write a few sentences explaining what T'aejo means and explain how his ideas conflicted with what many Koreans thought was the reason T'aejo was king.

_____

_____

_____

_____

_____

WORKING WITH PRIMARY SOURCES

Read the two quotations below. The first is from a Korean scholar. The second is from one of King Sejong's court historians. They were both written at about the same time. Then answer the questions.

I. It is said that when one makes a new ax handle, one examines an old one as a model, and that when one builds a new carriage, one uses an old carriage as a model. This is so we can learn lessons from the past.

II. No one seeing it does not heave a sigh and aver [swear] that we Koreans certainly had nothing like this in former times.

1. What is meant by the first quotation?

_____

_____

2. The second quotation was an observation of the water clock presented at King Sejong's court as a new invention. What point is the historian making in this statement?

_____

_____

_____

3. What does each statement say about the meaning of time?

_____

_____

_____

_____

RISE AND SHINE: RULERS AND TREASURE SHIPS IN MING CHINA

CHAPTER SUMMARY

The Ming dynasty was founded by Zhu Yuanzhang, who worked to improve life for the common person. Zhu Di became the next emperor and under his leadership China became a power in maritime trade and exploration. After the death of his admiral, Zheng He, maritime trade ended and China turned away from the world outside its borders.

ACCESS

What do you know about the history and culture of China? Write your ideas in the *Know* column of a K-W-L chart (see page 8 of this study guide). Then write questions you have about China in the W, or *What I Want to Know*, column of the chart. As you read the chapter, write answers and other new information in the L, or *What I Learned*, column of the chart.

CAST OF CHARACTERS

Write why each character was important.

Zhu Yuanzhang (joo yooan-jahng) _____

Zhu Di (joo dee) _____

Zheng He (jeng huh) _____

Fan Ji _____

WORD BANK

retaliation   epidemic   prosperous   regulation

Choose words from the Word Bank to complete the sentences. One word is not used.

1. The Black Death was an _____ that killed many people in Asia and Europe.

2. When the country was attacked, it acted in _____ by declaring a war.

3. The government _____ states that all children must attend school.

WORD PLAY

Look up in the dictionary the word that you did not use. Write that word in a sentence.

_____

WITH A PARENT OR PARTNER

Discuss the meaning of the word *prosperous* with a parent or partner. In your history journal, write the different forms of the word, such as *prosper* and *prosperity*. Discuss the meaning of these words and write a sentence using each form.

CRITICAL THINKING
SEQUENCE OF EVENTS

The sentences below describe events during the Ming dynasty. Put them in order by writing the sentence numbers in the correct order in the sequence of events chart below.

1. Ming Taizu improved the education system.

2. Zhu Di fought in a civil war and won.

3. Yongle sent Zheng He on a maritime expedition.

4. Zhu Di became emperor Yongle.

5. Zhu Yuanzhang named the dynasty Ming, meaning "brilliance."

6. It became illegal to build a ship with more than two masts.

7. Yongle built his new capital, Beijing, at the old Mongol capital of Dadu

8. Maritime trade helped China to become very wealthy.

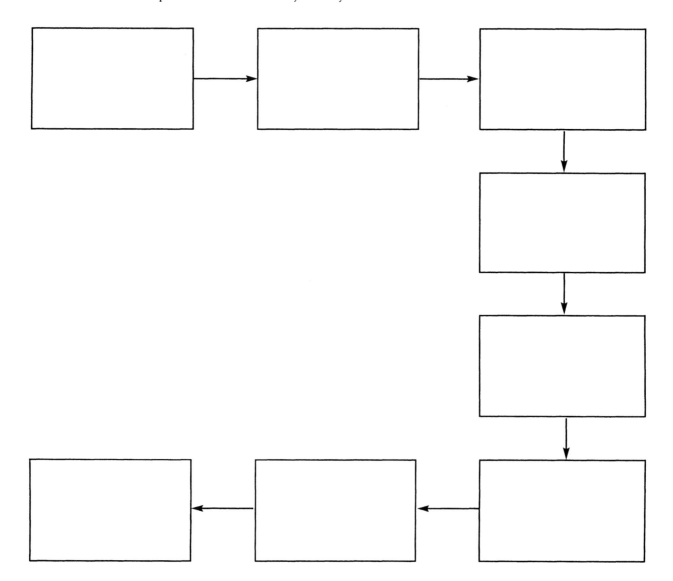

WORKING WITH PRIMARY SOURCES

Read the quotation from Ming Taizu to the teachers.

> Since you do not understand worldly matters and are unacquainted with conditions among the people, what do you regularly teach? Even if you had good students they would be ruined by you!

WRITE ABOUT IT

In your own words, write what you think Ming Taizu is trying to tell the teachers.

_____

_____

_____

WRITING

Write a few sentences explaining why Ming Taizu might have felt the way he did about the work the teachers were doing.

_____

_____

_____

_____

CRITICAL THINKING

COMPARE AND CONTRAST

The following words and phrases describe the reigns of Ming Taizu and Yongle. Organize them into the Venn diagram provided. Write the corresponding letter for all the words and phrases that describe Emperor Taizu in the circle labeled *Ming Taizu*. Write the corresponding letter for all the words and phrases that describe Emperor Yongle in the circle labeled *Yongle*.

a. belonged to Ming dynasty

b. was opposed to wars for expanding territory

c. relied on eunuchs as servants and advisers

d. built new capital

e. led expeditions against Mongols

f. established public schools

g. wanted to extend Ming influence overseas

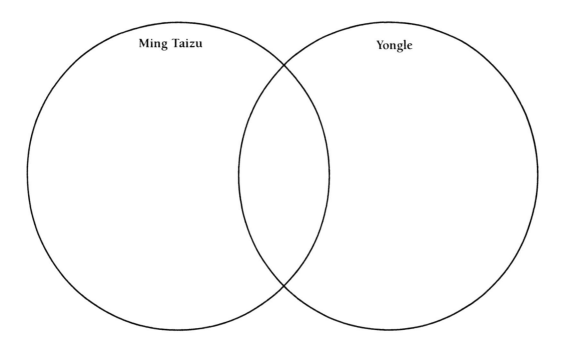

WORKING WITH PRIMARY SOURCES

Read the quotations below. Then answer the questions.

> . . . the expansion of territory is not the way to enduring peace, and the over-burdening of the people is a cause of unrest.
>
> > — Ming Taizu's [or Zhu Yuanzhang's] speech to his officials on October 13, 1371

> Now all within the four seas are one family. . . . Let there be trade on the frontier to supply the country's needs and encourage distant people to come.
>
> > — Emperor Yongle [or Zhu Di] remarking on the first expedition to the South China Sea and Indian Ocean in 1405

> Although he returned with wonderful, precious things, what benefit was it to the state?
>
> > — Liu Daxia, vice president of the Ministry of War, commenting on Zheng He's treasure voyages in 1477, as reported by Gu Qi Yuan in *Idle Talk with Guests*, 1617

1. Compare and contrast these quotations. How do the writers' ideas differ?

_____

_____

_____

2. What do you think might account for the difference in these writers' views?

_____

_____

_____

IN YOUR OWN WORDS

In the lines below, paraphrase each of the statements using your own words.

_____

_____

_____

_____

_____

_____

WRITE ABOUT IT

Imagine you are an official in Emperor Yongle's court. The court is having an informal debate about the risks and benefits of overseas trade. In your history journal, describe the scene and record the conversation that takes place. At the end, write down your own opinion, and why you think so.

HISTORY JOURNAL

Don't forget to share your history journal with your classmates, and ask if you can see what their journals look like. You might be surprised—and get some new ideas.

NAME _____

LIBRARY/ MEDIA CENTER RESEARCH LOG

DUE DATE _____

Brainstorm: Other Sources and Places to Look

Places I **Know** to Look

What I Need to **Find**

I need to use:

- [ ] primary } sources.
- [ ] secondary

WHAT I FOUND

Title/Author/Location (call # or URL)

How I Found it

- [ ] Suggestion
- [ ] Library Catalog
- [ ] Browsing
- [ ] Internet Search
- [ ] Web link

- [ ] Primary Source
- [ ] Secondary Source

- [ ] Book/Periodical
- [ ] Website
- [ ] Other

Rate each source from 1 (low) to 4 (high) in the categories below

helpful   relevant

NAME

LIBRARY/ MEDIA CENTER RESEARCH LOG

DUE DATE

What I Need to **Find**

I need to use:

- [ ] primary sources.
- [ ] secondary

Places I **Know** to Look

Brainstorm: Other Sources and Places to Look

WHAT I FOUND

Title/Author/Location (call # or URL)

How I Found it

- [ ] Suggestion
- [ ] Library Catalog
- [ ] Browsing
- [ ] Internet Search
- [ ] Web link

- [ ] Primary Source
- [ ] Secondary Source

- [ ] Book/Periodical
- [ ] Website
- [ ] Other

Rate each source from 1 (low) to 4 (high) in the categories below

helpful   relevant

NAME _____

LIBRARY/ MEDIA CENTER RESEARCH LOG

DUE DATE _____

Brainstorm: Other Sources and Places to Look

Places I **Know** to Look

What I Need to **Find**

I need to use:
- ☐ primary sources.
- ☐ secondary

WHAT I FOUND

Title/Author/Location (call # or URL)

How I Found it
- ☐ Suggestion
- ☐ Library Catalog
- ☐ Browsing
- ☐ Internet Search
- ☐ Web link

- ☐ Primary Source
- ☐ Secondary Source

- ☐ Book/Periodical
- ☐ Website
- ☐ Other

Rate each source from 1 (low) to 4 (high) in the categories below

helpful   relevant

NAME

DUE DATE

What I Need to **Find**

I need to use:

- ☐ primary
- ☐ secondary

sources.

Places I **Know** to Look

Brainstorm: Other Sources and Places to Look

WHAT I FOUND

Title/Author/Location (call # or URL)

How I Found it

- ☐ Suggestion
- ☐ Library Catalog
- ☐ Browsing
- ☐ Internet Search
- ☐ Web link

- ☐ Book/Periodical
- ☐ Website
- ☐ Other

- ☐ Primary Source
- ☐ Secondary Source

Rate each source from 1 (low) to 4 (high) in the categories below

helpful   relevant

Breinigsville, PA USA
06 July 2010
241278BV00002B/3/P